THE RIDER'S AIDS

by

Pegotty Henriques

Illustrations by

Carole Vincer

THRESHOLD BOOKS

First published in Great Britain by
Threshold Books, The Kenilworth Press Limited
Addington, Buckingham, MK18 2JR

© The Kenilworth Press Limited 1991

Typeset by DP Photosetting, Aylesbury, Bucks

Printed in Great Britain by Westway Offset

British Library Cataloguing in Publication Data

Henriques, Pegotty
    The rider's aids. – (Threshold picture guides)
    I. Title   II. Series
    798.23

    ISBN 1872082238

CONTENTS

Introduction

The aids are a system of signals, used by the rider to communicate with the horse and tell him what to do.

The aids are mostly a silent language of touch and feel.

As the horse progresses in his training the signals given by the rider become more complex and subtle. The basic aids should be straightforward and simple.

As the art of riding has developed over the centuries, so different systems of aids have evolved.

All classical systems have developed in the great cavalry schools of Europe and have stood the test of time. They are all proven, effective ways of communicating with a horse.

As long as the rider is consistent it is irrelevant which classical system he uses.

Those advocated in this book are the most commonly taught and used.

The riding scholar should understand all the systems for he may be called upon to ride a variety of horses trained in different ways.

The novice rider who wishes to convey the simplest of messages need not concern himself with such complexities, but should stick to the most basic aids.

It is only when classical systems become integrated that problems and confusion result.

The rider should at all times be clear in his own mind as to exactly how he wishes to convey a message to his horse. If he is consistently clear his horse will soon learn to understand.

Understanding the horse

For thousands of years the horse was a wild, free animal who ran in herds. He relied on his swiftness and his senses of smell, hearing and sight to protect him from the dangers of predatory carnivorous animals.

By nature he is not an aggressive animal and any action that appears so is purely defensive.

Modern horsemen have learned that, through kindness, it is easy to gain a horse's confidence. Once a horse learns that he can trust his rider he will do anything he is asked. If that trust is destroyed by, for example, asking him to jump obstacles that are too big and that frighten him, it will take a considerable time to re-establish his confidence.

Despite his looks, a horse is not a highly intelligent animal. He does, however, have a remarkable memory that

recalls situations and actions and associates them with pleasure and rewards, fear and pain. It is through our knowledge and understanding of the horse's memory that we have learned how to train him.

Riders often forget that the horse has to learn to understand their aids. It is not natural for him to stop when the reins are pulled or go forward when he is kicked. Quite the contrary, in fact.

Although he is capable of being lazy and disobedient, he also learns to respect and obey the rider who firmly insists that he does as he is told and then rewards him.

Quick, correct responses from the horse must immediately be rewarded with a kind word or a pat. A lack of response must equally quickly be corrected.

Sensitive areas of the horse

There are certain areas of the horse's body that are particularly sensitive and can easily be touched by the rider as he sits in the saddle.

Perhaps the most important of these is the area just beside the rider's heel. This area extends under the horse's belly and behind the rider's leg.

The flank is also sensitive, but of course can only be reached by the rider's whip.

The area beneath the saddle can feel the slightest change of pressure, and any shift of the rider's weight can influence the horse.

The whole area of the mouth and muzzle is highly sensitive and pain can easily be inflicted through rough use of the reins and the bit.

The ears listen to the rider's voice and, in their movement, express how the horse is thinking.

It gives horses great pleasure to be scratched or caressed just in front of the withers. You will often see two horses in the field scratching each other with their teeth for their mutual enjoyment.

Just as horses quickly learn to accept the uncomfortable burden of a rider on their back so, equally, they will learn to ignore the rider who constantly pulls at the reins or kicks with his legs.

Although many riders complain that their horse is insensitive, watch the way a horse responds to a fly landing on him!

It is riders who train horses to be insensitive with their incessantly and inaccurately applied aids. Horses quickly learn to tolerate a remarkable degree of discomfort.

These are the sensitive areas of the horse that are important to the rider and involve feel, hearing and sight.

Too many signals quickly confuse the horse to the point when he thinks it is better to ignore them.

The rider's position

The rider gives signals (applies aids) to the horse, principally with his lower legs, his hands and his body weight. He also uses his voice and, at times, a whip and spurs.

It is difficult for the beginner to give clear signals if he is out of balance. The first priority in learning to ride is to establish a balanced seat.

This is achieved when the rider sits centrally in the deepest part of the saddle, his body upright and his weight equally distributed on his two seat bones.

Seen from behind at the halt, an imaginery vertical line should run down the rider's spine, in line with the horse's spine and tail. His feet, hips, and shoulders should be level.

From the side, a vertical line should pass through the rider's ear, shoulder, hip and heel.

As the horse moves so the rider's body flows with the horse in a reciprocal way.

If he tries to hold on with his legs or becomes stiff and rigid the horse will receive many unintended signals, mostly to his mouth.

The rider absorbs the movements of the horse through his spine and hips. If he stiffens them he will bump uncomfortably in the saddle.

It is easy to understand why horses that carry many beginners on their backs learn to ignore odd kicks, bumps and pulls.

Riders need to develop control over certain muscles. Strength is seldom required.

A rider who is comfortably in balance with his horse will find riding relatively effortless.

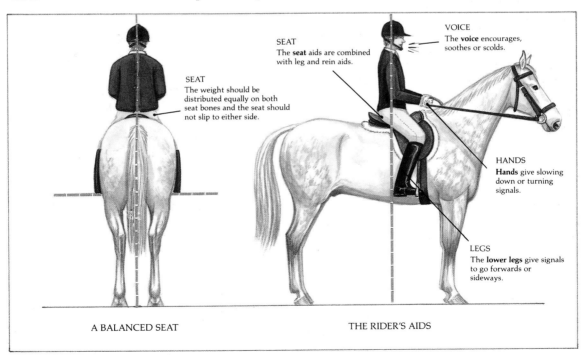

SEAT
The weight should be distributed equally on both seat bones and the seat should not slip to either side.

SEAT
The **seat** aids are combined with leg and rein aids.

VOICE
The **voice** encourages, soothes or scolds.

HANDS
Hands give slowing down or turning signals.

LEGS
The **lower legs** give signals to go forwards or sideways.

A BALANCED SEAT

THE RIDER'S AIDS

The rider's position (cont.)

The rider should settle himself in the deepest part of the saddle with his weight distributed equally on both his seat bones.

His upper body should be upright and not collapsed at the waist. His ear, shoulder, hip and heel should form a vertical line.

His thigh should lie softly against the saddle, allowing the weight of the leg to drop towards the ball of the foot and rest on the stirrup in a natural, unforced way.

The lower leg should rest against the horse's sides. The heel should be lower than the ball of the foot.

In walk the rider moves in harmony with the horse by pushing his tummy forwards and back.

In trot the rider may either remain sitting in the saddle, absorbing the movement of the trot with a similar movement to the walk, or he may rise.

In rising trot the rider takes his seat out of the saddle on the first beat of the trot, by half standing in his stirrups, then lowers his seat again on the second beat of the trot. This is considered more comfortable for both horse and rider. The sitting trot, however, allows the rider's seat to influence the horse more powerfully.

In canter the rider keeps his seat in the saddle and moves his upper body forwards and backwards without collapsing at the waist. If he locks his hip joint he will bump about uncontrollably.

When jumping and galloping the rider leans forward so that he is balanced over his feet with the weight of his seat out of the saddle.

The rider is taking the weight, through his knees, on the balls of his feet. He is balanced and able to keep an unvarying contact on the reins.

A novice rider, out of balance and behind the movement, is unable to control his hands because he has lost control of his body.

At all times the rider's hands should be carried so that there is a straight line from his elbow, down the back of his hand to the horse's mouth.

As the horse moves his head to and fro, the rider should keep the contact of the reins without variation. To do this he must move his elbow and shoulder joints.

He applies rein aids by squeezing his fingers. Small finger aids will only be effective if a good rein contact is kept.

The rider's lower leg should be in contact with the horse's sides with a light, equal contact.

Leg aids are applied where the leg normally lies and also well behind the girth, approximately two to three hands' breadth further back. The toe remains pointing forwards.

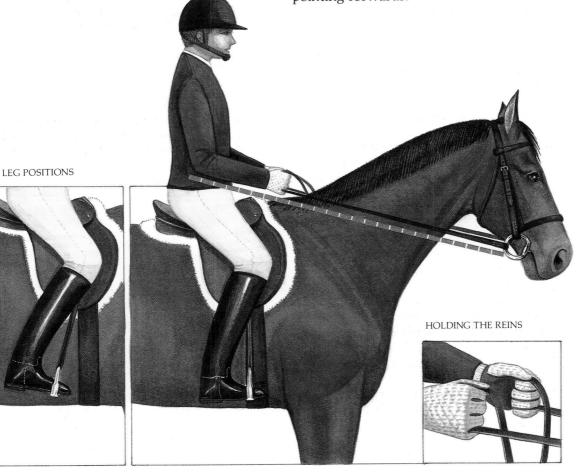

LEG POSITIONS

HOLDING THE REINS

The lower leg, either 'behind the girth' or in its normal position, can be applied with a sustained inwards pressure or a quick nudge.

The reins pass between the fourth and little finger, over the index finger and under the thumb. The nails should touch the heel of the palm.

Body weight

The novice rider should pay great attention to sitting centrally in the saddle with his weight equally distributed. Once the bad habit of crookedness has developed it is very hard to correct.

A crooked rider soon makes his horse crooked for the horse puts himself under the rider's centre of gravity and moves towards it.

Riders who are crooked often look as though their stirrup leathers are unequal. In fact it is more likely that they are sliding to the left or right and putting more weight in that stirrup.

The most common fault is sliding to the outside of the saddle as the horse turns or circles in the other direction. The rider collapses his inside hip and puts his weight in the outside stirrup. Leaning inwards is equally a fault.

The rider who always leans one way as he jumps will almost certainly have a horse that jumps crookedly. This can be used to the rider's advantage if, while in the air, he begins a right turn by leaning in that direction.

The good rider uses his weight when necessary as a subtle influence. It can be a powerful influence on the horse, especially at advanced levels. The weight is applied by pushing one or both hips slightly forward.

The rider who has an established habit of crookedness must first become equal and straight and only then consider the value of weight aids.

The permanently crooked rider not only has a paralysing effect on himself and his own ability to apply equal aids but also on his horse by making him one-sided and stiff.

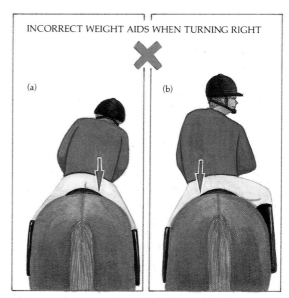

INCORRECT WEIGHT AIDS WHEN TURNING RIGHT

(a)

(b)

(a) Disturbing the horse's balance by leaning forwards and inwards. (b) Collapsing the right hip and sliding to the outside of the saddle.

JUMPING

This rider has put his weight to the left. His horse has already responded by preparing to land on the correct leg to make a left turn.

The rider's voice

The human voice plays a very important part in the training of the horse.

From his earliest associations with humans he will have learnt to interpret a variety of different tones of voice and connect them with feed time, pleasure or scolding. He will generally learn to come when he is called and to react to commands such as 'Stand still'.

As he grows older and his training on the lunge begins he will learn different commands such as 'Walk', 'Trot', 'Canter', 'Halt', 'Steady' and 'Good'. Once he is backed the verbal commands are converted into the system of physical commands we call 'the aids'. But for quite a long time those verbal commands back up the rider's aids and help the horse to understand what we want him to do.

At even the highest level of training there is no doubt that the use of the voice can please, calm and soothe, encourage or scold depending on how it is used.

The horse is very quick to pick up the rider's feelings and will respond to nervous or aggressive words.

The rider who panics and screams when his horse is frightened will increase his horse's anxiety. He can just as easily calm him with soothing words.

It is vital that the horse understands when he has done well. A 'Good' from the rider will please and encourage him. A growl will show displeasure.

It is important to use the same word with the same inflexion. It is the tone of voice to which the horse responds.

An attentive horse, listening to the rider's aids and voice, will often be seen to flick his ears back or even carry them slightly sideways.

A raised head and excessively pricked ears show a lack of attention to the rider. The combined use of leg and voice aids may regain his attention.

The beginner's basic aids

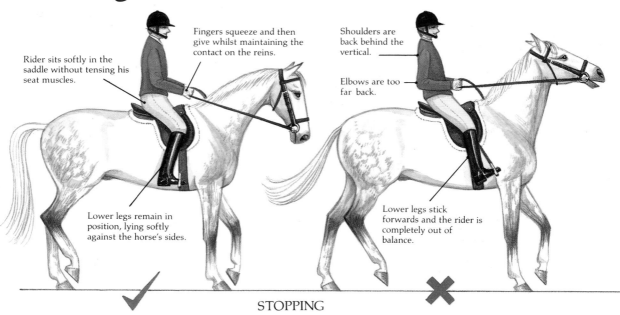

Rider sits softly in the saddle without tensing his seat muscles.

Fingers squeeze and then give whilst maintaining the contact on the reins.

Lower legs remain in position, lying softly against the horse's sides.

Shoulders are back behind the vertical.

Elbows are too far back.

Lower legs stick forwards and the rider is completely out of balance.

STOPPING

The first thing a beginner needs to know is **how to stop**.

His body should be upright, neither tipping forwards nor leaning back. His lower legs should rest against the horse's sides but he must not grip nor tighten. Feeling a contact with the reins he should squeeze his fingers briefly against his palms, momentarily increasing the tautness of the reins. He may need to repeat this squeeze-and-give before the horse fully understands. A soothing 'Whoa' or 'Halt' may help initially. Remember that every rider gives aids in a slightly different way and the horse must adjust to the slight change.

To move from halt to walk or trot the rider maintains a steady contact with the reins and gives a quick nudge inwards with his lower leg just where it lies. As the horse responds the rider must be careful not to pull backwards with his hands but to maintain the rein contact.

To turn to the left the rider must try to keep the weight equally on his two seat bones. His left leg should press inwards without the toe turning out and he should squeeze with his fingers to increase the contact on the left rein. As the horse begins the turn he will bend his neck in the direction in which he is turning. The rider must be careful to allow this movement by moving his right hand slightly forwards. The right rein must not, however, become loose and there must continue to be a contact between the rider's hand and the horse's mouth. If the right rein becomes slack the horse will probably bend only his neck to the left while he continues to move on a straight line without turning.

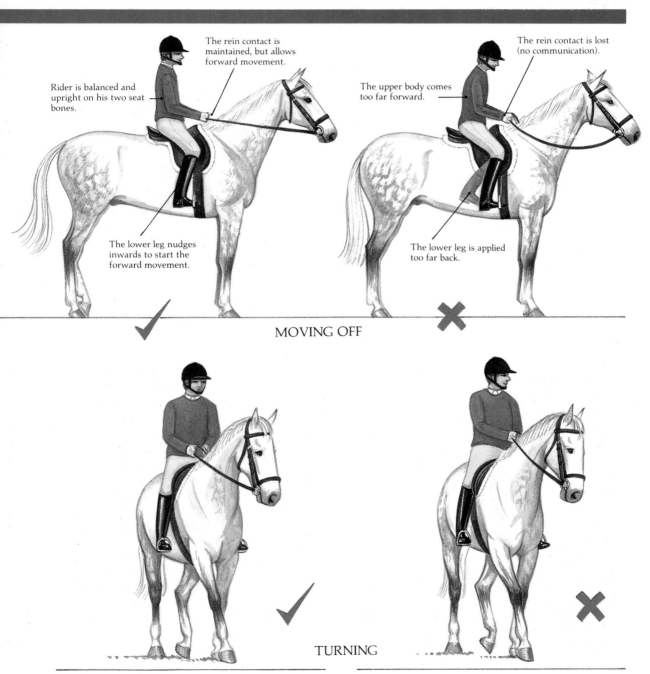

The rein contact is maintained, but allows forward movement.

Rider is balanced and upright on his two seat bones.

The lower leg nudges inwards to start the forward movement.

The rein contact is lost (no communication).

The upper body comes too far forward.

The lower leg is applied too far back.

MOVING OFF

TURNING

To turn to the left the rider should squeeze the left rein and press inwards with the left leg.

The rider is leaning inwards and crossing his right hand over the horse's withers.

The artificial aids

Spurs and whips are known as artificial aids.

Spurs should never be used by beginners or even novice riders as it is easy to misuse them if the rider loses balance and control of his legs.

Fitted so that the longest of the two metal arms is on the outside of the foot, the spur should point downwards. It should lie along the seam of the boot, with the buckle and end of the strap on the outside of the foot. The end of the spur should be rounded and smooth to avoid bruising. Only the inside edge of the spur should be applied to the horse's sides.

The whip or stick can more safely be used by the novice rider.

Schooling whips are quite long and can be applied behind the rider's leg without the rider taking his hand off the rein.

A schooling whip is too unwieldy for jumping so a shorter, jumping whip should be used. Its length necessitates taking the whip hand off the rein to use it.

The whip should not be used to inflict pain on the horse. It should be applied only as a sharp reminder when the horse fails to respond to the leg aids.

It is far better to back up an ignored leg aid with a sharp tap than to deaden the horse's sides by continual kicking.

The whip may be carried in either hand and should be changed as circumstances dictate. If the horse fails to listen to an aid from, for example, the right leg, then the whip should quickly be changed to the right hand to support that leg aid.

A correctly fitted and applied spur. The inside edge brushes against the horse's sides. Used in such a way it becomes a more refined aid.

Because the rider's toe is pointed outwards the back of the spur sticks directly into the horse's side. This could easily damage or bruise.

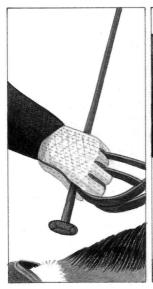

CHANGING THE SCHOOLING WHIP

The reins should first be taken into the whip hand. The whip hand should then rotate so that the whip is pointing directly upwards.

The free hand takes the whip and afterwards retakes the rein. A wise rider will pat the horse, to reassure him, before he changes the whip.

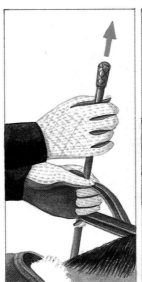

CHANGING THE JUMPING WHIP

The reins should be put into the whip hand, then the free hand draws the whip upwards through the palm and afterwards re-takes the rein.

Held with the tip pointing upwards the use of the whip is too forceful and is also a danger to the rider, who may poke himself in his eye.

Developing better aids

Once the very basic stop, start and turn aids have been understood and successfully used it is time for the rider to increase his vocabulary of aids.

This is only possible once the rider has developed a secure seat that is the result of confidence and balance rather than strength and rigidity.

As soon as the rider is assured and comfortable enough to stay in harmony with the different movements of the horse he should start to develop more refined aids.

The hands must learn to act independently of each other and in different ways. Equally the legs have to work individually. At first this is difficult.

The legs aids are applied in two ways:

- With a sharp inwards nudge.
- With increased inwards pressure.

The range of meanings is greatly increased when the positioning of the leg aids, applied in such a way, is varied:

- For increasing impulsion and forward movement the leg is applied where it lies with a quick inwards nudge.
- To make the horse bend (curve his body) the leg is applied where it lies and kept in firm contact with the horse's sides.
- Used further back behind the girth with a brief nudge it indicates canter strike-off.
- Used further back behind the girth and kept in contact with the horse's side it controls or moves the quarters.

Using leg and rein aids is a little like playing the piano. Your hands have to learn to do different things and so do your feet.

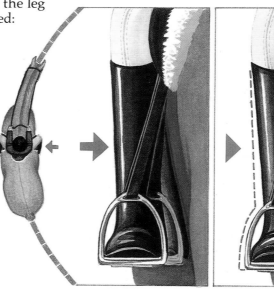

An inwards nudge of the leg, where it lies, asks the horse for increased energy (impulsion). Used with pressure it asks for bend.

The contact on the reins must be maintained without interruption. The rein aids are applied with a take-and-give squeeze of one or both reins.

The movement of the horse's head must be mirrored by the hands. In walk and canter there is considerable movement to and fro, in trot there may be some movement but it is unlikely to be regular. The horse also bends his neck to the left or right. Such movement must be allowed without losing the contact.

Although legs and hands must always be used in conjunction, the golden rule, 'Legs before hands' must not be forgotten.

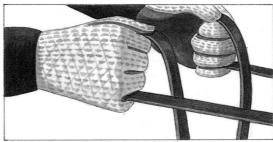

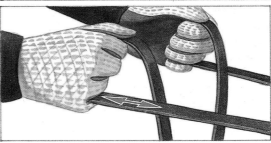

All rein aids are applied with a take-and-give (squeeze-and-give). The hand must never pull backwards or hold.

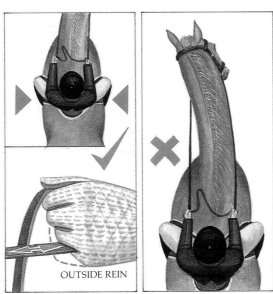

The outside hand controls the speed with a take-and-give. Pulling the outside rein will stop the horse bending and cause his head to tip.

INSIDE REIN   OUTSIDE REIN

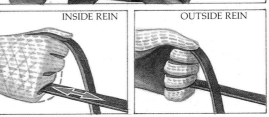

The inside rein, supported by the inside leg on the girth, asks the horse to bend or indicates the direction of a turn or circle.

The bend of the horse

The frequently used terms 'inside' and 'outside' need to be fully understood by the rider.

When a horse is being ridden to the right, the term 'inside' applies to the right side of the horse and the term 'outside' to the left side of the horse.

It is the rider's aim to make his horse bend to the inside, his body following the curve of the line on which he is travelling. If the circle is very large, the bend of the horse is very slight. When the circle is small, the bend is considerably greater.

Equally, the horse must bend in the direction of the turn.

The inside or outside rein or leg aids are constantly used terms and the rider should understand them as clearly as he understands left or right.

When a horse is travelling to the right, even if he is on the long, straight side of a manège, he is considered to be 'on the right rein', his right being the inside.

The inside leg is used on the girth with increased pressure to make the horse bend (away from the pressure). The inside rein gives a light 'take-and-give' to make the horse bend softly to the inside.

The outside rein plays a most important part in supporting the inside rein. Its constant, yet yielding contact stops the horse bending its neck to the inside. The outside leg, well back, stops the quarters swinging outwards when necessary.

Ideally the horse should accept a firmer contact with the outside rein than with the inside rein. As he progresses, the rider will learn to fully appreciate the value of the outside rein.

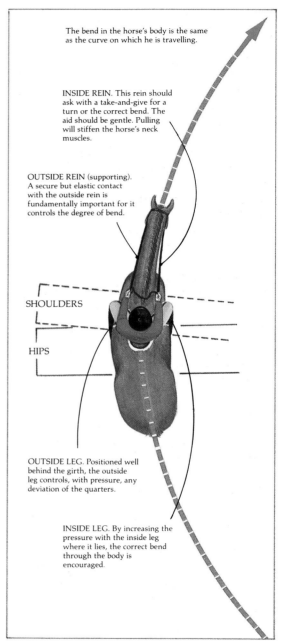

The bend in the horse's body is the same as the curve on which he is travelling.

INSIDE REIN. This rein should ask with a take-and-give for a turn or the correct bend. The aid should be gentle. Pulling will stiffen the horse's neck muscles.

OUTSIDE REIN (supporting). A secure but elastic contact with the outside rein is fundamentally important for it controls the degree of bend.

SHOULDERS

HIPS

OUTSIDE LEG. Positioned well behind the girth, the outside leg controls, with pressure, any deviation of the quarters.

INSIDE LEG. By increasing the pressure with the inside leg where it lies, the correct bend through the body is encouraged.

The rider's shoulders should be parallel with the horse's shoulders and his hips parallel with the horse's hips.

Aids to canter

A horse cantering to the right has a different sequence of footfalls to a horse cantering to the left. The rider needs to understand these before he seriously considers the aids to canter.

When travelling to the right the horse first puts his left hind to the ground. His right hind and his left fore then come to the ground together and finally his right fore comes to the ground. This last-placed leg is termed the 'leading leg'. The sequence is reversed when he canters to the left, with the left foreleg becoming the leading leg.

It is easier for the horse and the rider to start to canter on a named leg just before a corner.

To start cantering with the right leg leading, the rider should trot on the right rein and as a right-handed corner approaches he should ask for the correct bend with the inside leg and rein, sit softly in the saddle and brush his outside leg back, giving a nudge well behind the girth. The trained horse should strike off directly into canter.

On no account should the rider drop the contact on the reins as the horse would then only go faster and lose his balance. The rider must also resist the temptation to lean forwards and look down to check that he is on the correct leg. This unbalances the horse. The earlier the rider learns to depend on feel, the better.

A 'disunited canter', when the horse canters with the sequence of his legs muddled, is very uncomfortable and easily felt. The rider should return to trot and start again.

The rider's outside (left) leg has brushed back well behind the girth and the horse has begun the canter sequence with his left hind leg.

The same moment seen from behind. Note the rider's inside leg on the girth and the positioning of the horse's head to the right.

Turns and circles

The suppleness of the horse is increased by a variety of exercises on circles, turns and curved lines. These exercises will only be of value if they are ridden correctly.

To ride a circle the rider must decide two things:

- Exactly where the circle will begin.
- What size it is to be.

Any vagueness on the rider's part will result in unnoticed disobedience.

To ride a good circle the rider must prepare a few strides in advance of the starting point.

He makes sure that the horse is bent in the direction of the circle by using his inside leg and inside rein while keeping the contact of the outside rein. These are very subtle aids.

At the point where the circle begins the rider should look clearly in the direction to which he wishes to ride and increase the inside leg and rein aid. The outside rein plays an important part, for if the contact of this is lightened the beginning of the circle will lack precision. If, however, the rider's hand does not move forward to allow the horse's neck to curve to the inside the horse will be unable to bend correctly.

Once the circle is begun the rider needs only to ride forward and maintain the correct bend to ensure that the circle will be round.

The horse frequently avoids this suppling exercise by not bending his body and swinging his quarters out. The rider's outside leg behind the girth must correct any swinging of the quarters that might occur.

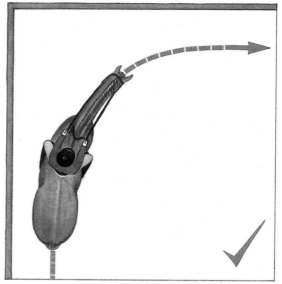

Turns should be ridden like quarter circles. This horse's body is correctly positioned. Note that the rider's outside hand allows the bend.

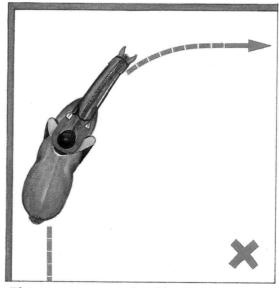

This turn is incorrectly ridden because the horse is not properly bent. His quarters are out and his neck is straight.

Horses should be worked equally on circles to the left and the right. Particular attention should be paid to the change of direction when the horse should momentarily be straightened, then bent in the new direction as the change of rein begins.

Although most horses have a stiff side they must learn to take the contact of the outside rein and not bend more one way than the other.

Faults to be avoided are:

- 'Falling out' – when the horse bends too much to the inside and drifts out on to his outside shoulder. Correct this by more contact on the outside rein and a firm outside leg contact.
- 'Falling in' – when the horse bends to the outside and leans inwards. Correct this by the strong use of the inside leg and a take-and-give of the inside rein.

'Falling in' – bent to the outside, with the weight being put on the horse's inside shoulder. The rider must apply strong corrective aids.

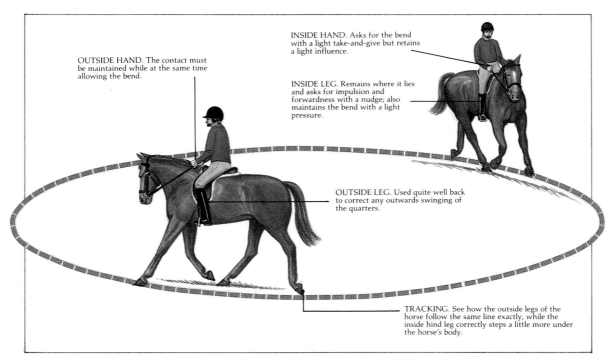

INSIDE HAND. Asks for the bend with a light take-and-give but retains a light influence.

OUTSIDE HAND. The contact must be maintained while at the same time allowing the bend.

INSIDE LEG. Remains where it lies and asks for impulsion and forwardness with a nudge; also maintains the bend with a light pressure.

OUTSIDE LEG. Used quite well back to correct any outwards swinging of the quarters.

TRACKING. See how the outside legs of the horse follow the same line exactly, while the inside hind leg correctly steps a little more under the horse's body.

Turn on the forehand

Making a turn on the forehand is usually the first lateral (i.e. sideways) movement that the rider is taught. It is an important exercise because it is the first time that the rider needs to use his legs and hands completely independently.

The turn on the forehand is done from the halt and at least 1½ metres (5 ft) away from the track or fence to allow turning space.

Ideally, after a square halt, the horse turns towards the track, his inside (track side) foreleg marking time and his hind legs making a half circle round his forelegs. One hind leg crosses over and in front of the other. The horse should: be bent in the direction he is turning; keep the walk sequence of steps; not step back.

To make a right turn on the forehand, the rider will start on the left rein. Riding in from the track he should begin with an attentive, square halt, then ask for a slight bend with the inside (right) rein. (When turning to the right, the right side of the horse becomes the new 'inside'.)

The outside rein stops the horse stepping forward but allows the slight bend. The inside leg, just behind the girth, asks the quarters to move over, and the outside leg, further back, is there to control the quarters when necessary.

As the turn is completed the forward aids should immediately be applied.

The rider should feel that he is controlling the horse's shoulders and keeping them still while his legs move the quarters around to complete the change of direction.

Turning right, the hind legs make a half circle round the forehand. The right foreleg moves on the spot, while the right hind leg crosses the left.

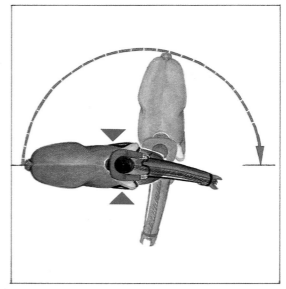

The right rein asks for bend while the left rein stops the horse moving forwards. The right leg moves the quarters; the left waits and receives.

Shoulder-in

Once the rider has mastered the turn on the forehand and can co-ordinate the independent use of his hands and legs, he can attempt the shoulder-in, one of the most valuable training exercises for both horse and rider.

Generally executed in trot, this exercise is also about the control of the horse's shoulders. In a turn on the forehand they are kept in one place, but in shoulder-in they are moved to the inner track while the quarters stay in position.

The horse must show a soft bend to the inside. He will travel on three tracks, or four when more advanced. His inside hind and outside foreleg will travel on the same track, while the inside fore and the outside hind travel on their own tracks. The exercise loses its value if the horse fails to bend.

It is easier for the rider to make a small circle in preparation for the shoulder-in as the horse will naturally balance himself and take slightly shorter steps. It is necessary to have a slightly more collected trot than the normal working trot.

If starting from a small circle or corner the horse should already be correctly bent for the shoulder-in. If beginning on the straight the rider should first ask for a soft bend to the inside (inside rein, inside leg).

The movement is begun when the rider brings the horse's shoulder off the track with the outside rein while keeping the soft bend with a light 'asking' contact on the inside rein. The inside leg on the girth maintains the impulsion and keeps the horse moving forwards and sideways down the track. The outside leg corrects.

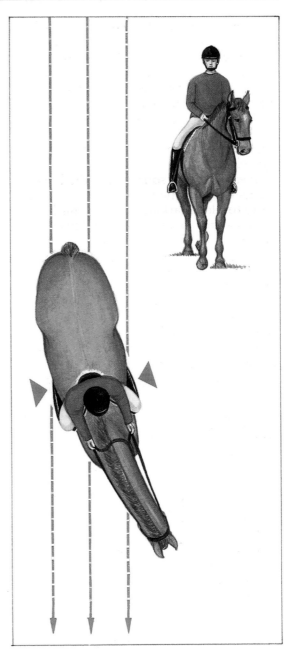

A three-track shoulder-in. Note the soft bend from the inside rein and leg and the important supporting outside rein contact.

Conclusion

By the time you have reached this page you may have discovered that the same aids seem, at times, to be applied for different reasons. This is true, but only partly so.

It is the subtle combination of legs, body weight and rein aids plus the minute variances that the rider develops that enable a wonderful partnership to unfold between him and his horse.

It is only when the rider is able to give light, almost invisible, aids that this advanced stage of communication can exist.

At first the rider will be searching for the right balance between leg and hand aids.

But from the beginning the rider should attempt to apply consistent, precise aids that will not confuse his horse.

The foundation of good aids is a good seat.

The basic aids should always be remembered:

- The inside leg applied where it lies asks for more impulsion or forward movement and also for bend.
- The outside leg well behind the girth controls the quarters and asks for the canter strike-off.
- The inside rein asks for bend and direction.
- The outside rein controls speed and bend. It is always supporting.

When the rider is able to use all these aids independently and without losing his balance, he is ready to use the added refinement of his weight aids. The influence of the rider's seat is from his seat bones. One or both hips are slightly advanced to momentarily increase the weight on one or both seat bones.

The rider should not confuse the horse by changing his system of aids but must remember that the horse learns through repetition because of his wonderful memory.

The rider, especially the novice, should never become angry when his horse apparently disobeys. Instead he should question his own actions:

'Was I clear?'
'Has he understood?'
'Is he capable of doing what I ask?'

If the answer to any of those questions is no then the fault lies with the rider.

If the horse is at fault, he may be inattentive, in which case the asking leg aid should be backed up by the whip. If he is nervous or anxious he should be calmed. The rider should *never* be rough with his hands.

In the beginning it seems very difficult to co-ordinate hand and leg aids. Gradually they become automatic reflexes; the rider finds that he has applied an aid almost without thinking about it. This is the most wonderful moment for he is developing the best aid of all: namely, 'feel'.

The rider is allowing his body to sense what his horse is doing rather than relying on his eyes and his brain.

He has become a horseman.